To Janet
Best wishes

Alvena
X

at the end of the rodden

Selection: Seán Body & Alrene Hughes

Design: Seán Body

Cover Photographs: Rose Morris

Manchester Irish Writers Logo
designed by Rose Morris

Acknowledgements
for Seán Body's poems are due to:
Poetry London Newsletter
& BBC Local Radio

Manchester Irish Writers wish to thank
the *Irish World Heritage Centre*
for its generous provision
of accommodation and facilities
for meetings and special events

and

Commonword for initiating this project
and for its continuing support

at the end
of the rodden

manchester
irish writers

Edited by
seán body

scríbhneoirí

First published 1997

Manchester Irish Writers

ISBN   0 9530072 0 0

supported
by

Commonword

Manchester Irish Writers
Irish World Heritage Centre
10 Queens Road
Manchester M8 8UJ

supported
by

north west
arts
board

CONTENTS

Mary McGonagle Johnson
Granny — 7
A Choice For Orla — 8

Finn Deloughry
The Kilfinane Bus — 12
In Memoriam Ger Nash — 13
Swan Song — 14
Famine Song — 22
My Irish Box — 23

Anna Brogan
Flying Colours — 25

Rose Morris
Homeless Family — 39
That Time — 40

Alrene Hughes
Aunt Kathleen — 41
Ballywalter — 42
A Missed Heartbeat — 43
An Irish Box — 53
In Gran's Kitchen — 54

Catherine Moloney
For James — 55

Catherine Breen
Coming Home — 56

Declan McCotter
Generations — 66
Death In The Country — 67
Parting Company — 68
Learning Irish — 69

Stella Marie Hinchcliffe
Pearls — 70
Metamorphosis — 72
Roots — 74

Seán Body
Bridges — 75
The Dart — 77
Mist Over Howth — 78
O'Connell Street — 79
The Mask — 81
Gertie — 95

MARY McGONAGLE JOHNSON

Mary McGonagle Johnson was born in Ballynahona, Malin, Co. Donegal. She is married and has lived in Manchester for about thirty years, but visits Malin several times a year.

A teacher by profession, she started writing about six or seven years ago. She has had two short stories published and has been short-listed for *The Irish Post Short Story Competition* on a number of occasions.

GRANNY

Granny why do you lie there in that strange brown box
    Why are you saying your prayers
    Why are your hands so cold Granny
    Your lips are saying no words

    The candle flickers on your face
    So white, and cold, and still
    Should I blow it out Granny
    Or would that be like a sin

    Why don't you speak or smile Granny
    Are you really very cold
    Would you like you're nice warm blanket
    The one that's bright and bold

They're pushing me out of the way Granny
    They're closing the lid on the box
    I scream but they don't hear me
    As they carry you out in that box

A CHOICE FOR ORLA

Slowly, the horizon faded as the ship built up speed in the gathering dark. Orla watched it disappear. The words from some old song she'd heard her grandfather sing came to her mind. A song about parents and lovers standing on the quayside, as their loved ones sailed out. She had mocked then, "You won't see me shed a tear. I can't wait to see the back of this one horse town." She and her friends had dreams of finding exciting jobs in England, as soon as they had finished their degrees. Jobs that paid good money, with which they would buy nice clothes.

Clothes were the last things on her mind as she stood on deck, watching the fading lights of the harbour. The easy confidence with which she had expressed her ambitions, only a few weeks before, had left her now. She was going to London, yes, but the excitement with which she had once anticipated that journey was replaced with dread. She wished she could have gone by plane, but as a student, she could not afford the fare and could not risk asking her parents; they might ask questions.

Orla looked vulnerable, as she stood looking out to sea; her long hair lifted by the breeze, her slight figure silhouetted against the fading light. She was glad to be on her own, to be able to relax without thinking that people might be scrutinising her. She had begun to look anxiously in mirrors, convinced that it was showing, even when she was only a month late.

The cold sea breeze sent a chill right through her. She was glad she had brought the Aran sweater her mother had knitted for her to take to university. She wrapped it tightly around her body, burrowing deep into the sleeves: a small frightened animal seeking comfort.

A few people were wandering about on deck. A young couple wrapped in each other, oblivious. A woman trying to comfort a small child. A man staring out to sea. Orla leaned out over the edge; it was cold down there. She shuddered.

The movement of the boat was making her nauseous. She decided to go inside. As she waited for a toilet to become vacant, her attention was taken by a woman who was changing a nappy. The baby objected strongly at first, then began to gurgle happily. It was looking at Orla, curiously.

The sickness welled up in her and she rushed into the toilet. When she came out, she was relieved to find they had gone. She decided to go to the cafeteria, a cup of tea might help. The cafeteria was filling up already. She looked around for a free table and sat down, well away from the others.

Everything had happened so quickly since she discovered she was pregnant. She felt in a spin, dazed. At first she could not believe it. It was not as if she had been careless. She was intelligent, knew how to avoid situations like this. So when the doctor confirmed her fears, she was horrified, ran out into the rain; walked around for hours in it, unable to go home. But, a couple of days later, when she was able to consider it more calmly, she decided it need not ruin her life. She was too young to have a baby. She would go to England: women had a choice there.

She rang a friend, in London, who advised her to come immediately. Luckily, the end of year exams had just finished. She could go at once and be back before anyone missed her.

She hoped things would happen quickly once she got there. Her boyfriend need never know. If he knew, he would want to marry her, try to persuade her. But she felt too young to settle down; they were both too young. She would handle it her own way. Any guilty feelings she felt, were quickly pushed aside in her preparations for the journey.

Once on the boat, she had felt a sense of relief. The strain of keeping her secret had begun to show, she felt tense and slept badly.

When she had finished her tea, she found a more comfortable seat and soon drifted off to sleep. She dreamt she was in a cold, white room. The cold made her shiver. There were several garda in the room; they were staring at her. She was wearing only the skimpiest of nightdresses and her stomach stuck out like a gigantic balloon. One of the garda prodded it with his baton. "Move up you tramp," he ordered, marching her up and down in front of the others. Each one in turn prodded her as she passed. She tried to plead, "You'll kill my baby, please don't kill my baby."

She became aware of loud shouting. Raised on a gallery, women were angrily waving their fists. "Murderer!" they were screaming, "Murderer!" In the background, Father O'Reilly's voice boomed, "Every child has the right..."

She felt trapped. There was no escape. Cold sweat was running down her face, down over her stomach, swamping her in a cold terror. A door opened. She ran towards it and was just about to escape when James, her boyfriend, appeared; he stood in the doorway, blocking her. "Please," she was pleading, "please..." But the words would not come. The shouting had stopped. Now it was only James; James in the doorway, white faced, uncovering the bundle he was carrying, handing it to her.

The baby's face was white, cold marble.

Her scream choked.

She felt someone touch her. "You alright, Dear?" the voice was asking gently, "Alright now?" The kindly arm around her, coaxing softly, "Alright...?"

Orla looked down at her hands, expecting to see the dead baby. She could still feel its cold weight. She was trembling and the tears were streaming down her face.

The woman was putting a coat around her, drawing it tightly around her shoulders. "You keep warm," she was saying, "You keep warm now. I'll get you a nice cup of tea."

She was still not fully awake; the light hurt. She lay down again and drew the coat over her head. She was trying to blot out the dream.

"You'll feel better with this inside you." The woman was back. Orla sat up and looked around. Dawn was breaking. The tea was warm and sweet. A sense of relief came flooding back. It had only been a dream; she looked around to reassure herself. Only a dream. "I'm fine now," she thanked the woman, "I'll just take a walk."

She drew the sweater tighter, and went out on deck. Standing there, watching the dawn come up, the sense of relief she had begun to feel, was evaporating again. In its place was beginning an even greater confusion, a deeper turmoil.

FINN DELOUGHRY

Finn Deloughry was born in Cork, but brought up in Limerick, which he regards as his home town. Educated there and in London, he has recently taken early retirement from teaching - to catch up on his reading.

He lives in Droylsden, near Manchester.

THE KILFINANE BUS

Everything has altered: nothing changed.
The road goes where it always went,
Naming its way with townlands
I took with me to England
As mnemonics of associations,
Until I could not remember
Without recalling him or her
Who gave it special feature.

We grew beyond each other and apart,
Cancelling the destinations
We briefly thought we held in common.
Then the hedges grew beyond recognition
And the road was re-surfaced
For the next generation
Of inseparable and sundered friends.

IN MEMORIAM GER NASH

With time between school and tea,
You were regularly into the fields
To check the seasons held to schedule;
That buds were budding, birds nesting;
The sloe, the haw, the crab apple
Were keeping promises, hedge to hedge.

And it is not true you sang to yourself—
You were never that self-centred—
For everyone who was out could hear,
Recognise the voice and call a greeting
To be answered as by nature;
Or, indeed, not interrupt at all
For what moved them in your song:
Down by the glenside I met an old woman,
So that now you and she blend
As one image in an Irish picture I preserve
Since, like yourself, Ger, I became
Live cargo... ready fledged to fly.

What resonances had your trees and fields
In the Black Country, Ger?
Two lifetimes and your death between us,
You lie in a Birmingham graveyard—
The city whose bins you emptied
And not *six stalwart warriors to carry me*
With steps that fall mournful and slow—
And the chilling irony of it is
That one of your favourite fields, Ger,
Is now adopted for a buryin' ground,
Where Limerick steals into your countryside.

SWAN SONG

He'd be better off the road. There should be a wall up there, a few hundred yards, which he could climb over for the path down to the river. He should not have forgotten. It used to be the much-visited haunt of children and courting couples. He had been there, in both capacities, in the distant past.

The memory still hurt, like an unrighted wrong or an arbitrary reversal of hope.

There was the wall, closer than memory estimated. Measurements seemed to have contracted, widths not as wide, distances not as great. Time not endless. He was judging all by a small boy's scale, just as in England he had found his initial responses to some events to be in the inappropriate moral currency.

The wall was more lichened and mossed. A few feet inside it, the ground sloped down, as of old. This was where it had amused her to watch him muscle their bikes, in turn, down to the lower level of the field, lay them on the ground and return to help her descend.

Receiving her into his arms in this way was her limit to any 'physicals', as she called them. Always, she drew back from where he would have had her linger. The momentary intimacy of that summer-frocked contact was his first discovering hint of maturity.

The path had disappeared, where it had made its sandy way between young hawthorns, now it was overgrown by the dense copse into which they had matured. People had long since ceased to come here, evidently. No alternative path skirting the copse had been worn and a wide detour was necessary to pass it and approach the riverbank. Their customary place, he saw, was part of the wilderness. Untrammelled nature had encroached and obliterated it.

She chose to sit here, clearly visible from the road above. He would not be tempted to engage in 'physicals'. He smiled at that usage. She gave the word a pre-emptive nuance. He was permitted to take her hand while they walked in the shelter of the path but she always disengaged it, when they reached the open again.

This had been their practice for three summers. Otherwise, they met briefly after school, among friends. On Saturday evenings, they went to the novena together.

He asked her once if it bothered her that she might be said to be going behind her parents' backs.

"We do no harm," she dismissed.

There was sophistry in her argument. The very fact of their being there was the 'occasion'. The doctrine did not allow for such fine distinctions.

"We do no harm," he conceded.

"You are considerate to ask. A girl...," she failed to finish.

"Appreciates?"

He chose not to pursue the topic further. He might give her cause against future meetings.

Out in the water, horizontal fronds of weed waved in the sluggish currents. Only the faithful pairs of swans gave him any hint of permanence.

"Do you know how many swans I can count from here?"

"Twenty? "

"Seventeen."

"One has lost a mate."

"That was unfeeling," for once angry.

"I didn't mean to sound cynical. I expect to find them in pairs at this time of the year," he defended. For the remaining afternoons, they made a repeated census of the swan population along this reach. It seemed to become her sole purpose. Their counts were never in agreement.

"My remark about the odd swan still rankles."

"What makes you say that?"

"You've seemed a little distant, since."

"It made you sound coarse," she admonished.

"What would make amends?"

She looked at him steadily and then, with a mischievous smile ordered, "Tomorrow be able to recite *The Wild Swans At Coole.*"

"I can do it now."

"You know it!"

"Don't sound so surprised."

They both found it funny.

"Does that cancel all suspicion of coarseness?" he teased.

"Smug, then."

"Know you've lost, when you have to resort to personal abuse."

"Oh, you cheeky devil," she pouted in feigned offence, pounding playfully on his chest. She stood close, breathing heavily but not from her exertions. Even then, he did not dare the embrace she tempted. With that hesitation, the moment passed.

He walked back to the wall and climbed out on to the verge. The one who got here first waited for the other.

One afternoon they met in town. Like a hosting, all their exact contemporaries gathered at their particular corner on the main street. They came from the directions of their various schools, some glum, most happy, with their exam results. He was standing with a group of their mutual acquaintances, when he saw her cycling up with uncommon abandon. He stepped forward to greet her.

"Your satisfaction is obvious. Congratulations."

"And you?" she asked, excited.

"Much better than I expected."

"Thank God," she beamed and then she was among the others and coming back to say "Isn't it great!" and sweeping off to enquire of still others.

"I want to congratulate you properly," he smilingly commanded.

Stilled for a moment, he was able to plant a light, chaste kiss on her cheek. "That's a thank you for your support," he grinned. She looked surprised but showed no sign of offence.

"Thank you," she murmured. Shrieks of pleasure ensued as the other boys took their cue from him. Then everybody went exchanging modest pecks.

She, he happily noted, joined in the festivities. During the milling scramble, they came face-to-face again. This time, she made it her occasion to kiss his cheek.

"Are you as happy as I am?"

"Happier."

"Impossible," he heard, as someone swept her away again.

While his eyes were still on her, a lubricious kiss was pressed on his lips. It was 'The Crow', as the boys called her. Clinging to him, she hissed, "She looks almost human, for once. You're wasting your time. Utterly self-centred. See you," she called and was gone back into the melee.

Unusually, they went that evening to their special place. Their elation had not entirely subsided. He held her hand and she skipped and danced beside him.

"This is the kind of occasion people celebrate by getting drunk, isn't it?"

"You're intoxicated by success, as it is!" he mocked and she responded with a little chortle of merriment. He raised her arm and required her to pirouette.

"The music is in my soul," he bowed and she made a curtsey. Yet, when they emerged from the cover of the path, she withdrew her hand.

"Who gave The Crow her nickname?" she asked unexpectedly.

"She was known by that before I got to know her. Why do you ask?"

"I was told what she did today. I didn't see it."

"You were otherwise engaged," he teased. "Did your informant put any interpretation on it?"

"No. We all know what a crush she has on you."

"Do we...all?"

"You know very well. It's a matter for everyone's amusement."

"I don't like to discover I'm a figure of fun."

"You're pretending again. If you must know, people admire the way you....are careful not to hurt her feelings, when she's being a bit obvious. Well, the girls notice. The boys never would."

"Do you find her amusing?"

"Don't ask."

"In case you incriminate yourself?"

"Don't flatter yourself," she laughingly taunted. Then she asked, "Are you ever tempted to go with her?"

"I'm not attracted."

"Even for the experience?"

"Boys' imaginations."

"Is that all it is, her reputation?"

"I know my friends."

"And yourself?"

"A sceptic."

"I begin to think you are too worldly-wise," she frowned.

"I don't anticipate, whatever I may know."

She stopped. "Don't ever forget how deeply it is appreciated."

"We should turn back before it gets cold."

For three afternoons, she did not come. On the morning of the fourth day, he went into town. Friends greeted him but did not stop. Was he foolish to think he sensed an atmosphere?

The Crow materialised before him. Her appearance was that instantaneous. She scrutinised him in anticipation, her dark eyes under her raven fringe, her thin, slightly beaked nose thrust upwards, as if in expectation of an augury.

"God, she was the secretive one. So were you."

"You seem to know something I don't," was all he could muster.

"You can stop the pretence, now she's gone."

"Gone where?"

"Oh God, she hasn't! You don't know? Oh, I wouldn't have said, if I'd realised. I am sorry."

Others of their friends began to gather, sheepishly, their expressions funereal.

"She didn't even tell him," she announced.

"Will somebody enlighten me?"

"She's entered the convent," pierced The Crow.

Taking his hands from the top of the wall, he straightened up. "Don't ever forget how deeply it is appreciated," he recalled.

FAMINE SONG

A presence pervades the place,
Threading like a leitmotif
Through its narrative weave;
Unmistakably herself
Yet temporally transformed
On each new appearance;
New-patterned, metamorphosed
To a vision of the latest generation,
As maid, as mother
Or the *old dear* who lays us out—
The feminine trinity by whom
Even the patriarchs are awed.

We would have her go away
Yet we detain her,
Summon her from absence
For want of an adequate image, symbol,
When we have lost the essence of ourselves.
We trace her from such as Knowth
Or Grange by Lough Gur
Where we stonily tied her to the sun
And, in most attenuated form,
Her voice is in the latest pop-song,
Lingering residually in the tune
Loaned, blackened and retrieved.

The last time she was seen for certain,
She walked on hungry grass above a mass grave
And gave her departing children their last sight.
Then those who stayed, with guilt of survivors,
Retired her to heritage centre and museum,
Not for a continuing reminder
But in pursuit of a catchpenny theme.

MY IRISH BOX

Imagine it Pandora's jar,
All woes escaped;
Its few remaining solaces
Fortuitously contained,
Clamped shut in panic;
Its contents treasured
Because they are worthless
Outside attributing imagination's
Scale of values.

It holds the sensate
And the numinous,
The immanent
And, if tangibles, only
For their associations;
Such stored realities
As the plash of lazy oar
On lambent Shannon
When the elvers ran
Under reddening sun
And with Martin and Denis
I laid down the vintage
Of a memorable summer.

It contains, as well,
The pearled gossamer
Of spiders' webs
In my sister's misted garden,
Droplets of redolence;
The heady scents,
Aromas, smells
Of heavy-uddered cows
At milking time,
Later that same warmed day.

There, too, memory's video
Of sighting Maeve
On the slope of Knockadoon,
Twice, for they are reflected
In the silent mirror of Lough Gur,
One eternal Sunday afternoon.

These have musical accompaniment,
They must,
Of monks at vespers
But yet,
Respecting stillness,
Contracting distances.

ANNA BROGAN

Anna Brogan was born in Donemana, Co. Tyrone. She started her teaching career in Birmingham, then, on her marriage in 1962, moved to Manchester. Her husband is a native of Donegal. They have three children. She is a member of Manchester Irish Players' Drama Group.

FLYING COLOURS

I was five years old, crouched on the kitchen floor, rolling marbles along the linoleum. If I managed to make the marble stop inside a square, I was a winner.

I was listening to my aunt and my mother talking. My aunt said, "Lizzie, I just can't get that cluckin' hen to sit on the eggs." My mother said, "Well, that's a quare pity. If she carries on like that, you'll not have wan wee chick out of that sittin' of eggs."

As I rolled my marbles, I thought it was a quare pity too. I looked at my aunt and said, "Can I sit on the eggs?" I waited until my aunt and my mother stopped laughing, then I said, "Well, can I?" My mother said, "Sure you'd be far too heavy, you'd flatten the wee chicks." While I was thinking what wee flat chicks would look like, my aunt said, "But if you would come up with me and stay for a while, you would be great company for your granny and your uncle Pat and me."

My mother said, "What do you think of that, Anna, do you want to try it for a while to see if you like it?" I wasn't too sure what I should think of it, but I said, "Aye, I'll try it for a while to see if I like it." My mother put some of my clothes in a bag. Then she handed me my schoolbag. When we were leaving, she patted me on the back and said, "Be a good girl now, I'll be up to see you soon."

My aunt held my hand as we walked up the road from my home. When we reached the top of my granny's lane, my aunt said, "And you'll be nice and near the school." The minute she'd said that, I felt scared and wanted to run back home, but it was dark and I was afraid of the dark. I was afraid of the teacher too. She used to keep hitting us with a small, thick, yellow stick if we made mistakes in our numbers or letters.

I walked on down the lane to my granny's door. My aunt went in first. I walked behind her and stood in the middle of my granny's kitchen floor, looking at my granny. My aunt said, "Anna's going to stay with us for a while, to see if she likes it." My granny looked straight at me, she had a big smile on her face. "That's great news," she said, "it'll be nice to have a young one around the house to keep us company." I stood there, in the middle of my granny's kitchen floor, I didn't know if it was great news or not.

Jim, my granny's dog, had been lying on the sofa, beside her. He kept looking at me. Then he started to rise up. He slid his back legs off the sofa and walked towards me. He kept looking at me and licked my hand. He had lovely shiny brown eyes. I knelt down in front of him and began to stroke his head. "Aye," I said, "I'll stay for a while, to see if I like it."

"The porridge's ready," my granny said, "give her some." My aunt took a wee blue dish from the dresser and went over to a big black pot that was hanging on a big black crane above the turf fire. The black pot had three legs. My aunt put porridge into the blue dish. Then she put milk and plenty of sugar on top of the porridge. She laid the blue dish on the table and a spoon beside it. "Sit over to the table now," she said. The porridge was so tasty I never wanted it to finish.

While I was eating the porridge, my granny said to my aunt, "You'll never believe it, that cluckin' hen has never budged off the eggs." I looked at my aunt, she had a big smile on her face. "Well, that's great news," she said. I thought it was great news too, my aunt would have wee chicks and I would see them.

I followed my aunt upstairs to the bedroom. I could see a small bed near the window and a big bed over near the back wall. My aunt pointed to the small bed and said, "That's your granny's bed, she has to be near the window. We have to leave it open a bit, so that she can breathe." I felt sad that my granny had something wrong with her and couldn't breathe, because she had smiled at me and had said that it was great news that I was coming to stay for a while to see if I liked it.

I jumped into the other bed to see what it was like. It was very soft. I said to my aunt, "This bed is lovely and soft." My aunt said, "It's a feather bed. Get undressed and get into it and I'll be up in a minute." I got undressed and got in. Then I rolled about in this lovely feather bed: I had so much room to roll about in. At home, I slept with my two sisters. They were older and used to push me to the very edge of the bed. "You'll push me out," I used to say to them, but they would only shout, "Shut up and go to sleep."

When my aunt got into bed, she put her arm around me. I felt safe. I lay there, waiting to go to sleep. Suddenly, I heard a little tapping noise on the ceiling. I looked up but couldn't see anything. I nudged my aunt and said, "What's that noise up there?" She was yawning and then said, "That's nothing, it's just the wee mice up in the rafters having a race." I kept on listening and wondered if the mice were lining up to have another race. I was right, because just then I could hear them racing. They seemed to be running very fast and then everything went quiet. I wondered if the same mouse won every race, would the other mice give up and refuse to run any more.

That must have been what happened, because there wasn't another sound.

The next morning, I woke up and for a minute I didn't know where I was. Then I remembered that I had come to stay at my granny's for a while to see if I liked it. My aunt walked with me to the school gate. She said, "After school come down the road with your sisters and you can come down the lane by yourself."

A bell rang and we all walked slowly into our classrooms. As soon as I looked at the teacher, the scary feeling came back. She was very, very old and always wore black clothes. She had grey wiry hair. It was pulled tightly back into a bun. She had a long sharp pin sticking out of it. She wore tiny glasses with silver round the edges of the glass. She always kept the glasses resting on the point of her nose and would stare at us over the top. She had very grey eyes. I didn't know anyone else who had grey eyes. Her grey eyes were very angry eyes.

We sat in our seats. She threw our books on to our desks and we started our writing practice. I had just started, when she rapped me on the knuckles with her thick yellow stick. I felt the pain and wanted to cry, but knew I mustn't, because she would rap my knuckles again and shout, "Stop crying!" She moved away from me and I watched her hitting other children. They never cried either. She was always hitting her own son: she hit him very hard. He would put his sore hand under his other arm and would look up at her. His face would be very red and sad, but he would not cry either. I was sorry for him. I was glad she was not my mother.

After the writing practice, the teacher would shout, "Who made you?" and we would all shout back, "God made me." Then she'd shout, "Why did God make you?" and we'd shout, "To know Him, love Him and serve him and by that means gain everlasting life." Then she'd yell, "Say the Ten Commandments." And we'd shout out the Ten Commandments. We all knew them off by heart. I didn't know what all the words meant, but I did know the meaning of two Commandments - fifth, *Thou shalt not kill* and seventh, *Thou shalt not steal.*

I knew about killing. When wasps were flying about, I would get a jam-jar that had a bit of jam left in it. I would put the jam jar near where there were some blackberry bushes and the wasps would fly into the jar. I would quickly screw the lid on tight and then I would watch them go lazy and die. I enjoyed watching them die.

Seventh, *Thou shalt not steal.* I used to steal pennies out of my mother's purse and buy sweets. Sometimes, when I was sent for a message to the shop near my home, the shopkeeper would be upstairs. That was where she lived with her very old mother. When I opened the door, a bell would tinkle on the door, but before the shopkeeper could get down the stairs, I knew I had time to run behind the counter and steal some dolly mixtures from the sweetjar.

The teacher told us that if we didn't do what the Commandments said, God would be very sad. She said if we were very bad, we would have to go to Hell. She said Hell was full of fire and we would burn forever. But God would give us a chance, if we told the priest, in our First Confession, about the bad things we did. The priest would ask God to forgive us. She said if we were very, very good we would go to Heaven when we died. She said Heaven was a beautiful, happy place and we would never be sick or sad again.

I couldn't wait to go to Confession, but I couldn't go until I was seven. That was a long time for me and I couldn't stop thinking that God must be very angry with me for killing wasps and stealing money and dolly mixtures.

Every day, the teacher talked about Hell. I kept wishing she would stop, but she never forgot to talk about it.

Just before the end of the school day, the teacher would say, "Protestants, go home." About ten boys and girls would stand up and walk out of the room. I thought it would be nice to be a Protestant, I could get out of school early. One day, just after the Protestants had walked out and before we began practising our prayers, the teacher said, "Isn't it very sad? Those Protestants are lovely children but they'll never get into Heaven." I didn't know why they wouldn't get into Heaven but I felt so sad I wanted to cry. A girl called Doris was my best friend, she was a Protestant and if Doris didn't get into Heaven, I didn't think I wanted to go there either. If Heaven was a very happy place, then I needed Doris, my best friend, to be with me.

After school, we would all run down the school lane, shouting and screaming. It was a great feeling to be able to scream and shout because all day in school we had to be silent, except when the teacher asked a question. I ran with my sisters to the top of my granny's lane. I started running down the lane. I stopped and looked back, my sisters were gone.

I walked slowly into my granny's house, she smiled at me and said, "There's a lovely herrin' for your dinner." I started picking the bones from the herring and laid them in a little row on the oilcloth. There were sixteen little thin bones. I counted them again to make sure. My granny said, "You're taking a long time to eat your herrin'. My aunt said, "Will you leave her alone? Can't you see she's picking out the bones. Did you eat the bones?" I looked over at my granny, she was eating a bowl of rice. I was glad because I liked my granny: she was glad I had come to stay with her for a while to see if I liked it. I knew the rice would cover up the bones she'd eaten, and the bones would not hurt her.

After dinner, I went for a walk outside my granny's house. I went into the henhouse. Up on a shelf, a hen was sitting on a nest. I knew it must be the cluckin' hen, because there was no other nest. I was glad the hen wasn't budging from the eggs, because I could never have sat away up there.

I went down to the bottom of granny's garden. There was a big flax mill there. I knew it was called a flax mill, because when I used to visit my granny's on Sundays, my sisters would say, "There's the flax mill."

"What's a flax mill?" I would ask, but they would only say, "You're too young. You don't understand."

Now I saw there were lots of men and women pushing something into big machines. There was dust everywhere. A man came out of the flax mill, I saw it was my uncle. I said, "What are they all doing in there?" He said, "They're pushing the flax into the machines and when the cover comes off the flax, there's lint."

"What's lint?"

"Lint is stuff that's turned into linen. The lint is put into a big dam of water and soaked for days. When the lint is in the dam, a lot of men and women take their shoes and socks off and tramp all over it until it softens. After a few days, there's an awful smell but that means the lint is ready to be turned into linen."

"What's linen?"

"Irish linen is great stuff. When the lint is laid out in the sun it becomes bleached white. Your granny has Irish linen tablecloths and they started as the flax that was brought to this flax mill."

That evening, when my uncle finished his dinner, he reached up to a shelf above the fireplace and took down something long. "What's that?" I asked.

"It's a gun," he said.

"What're you going to do with a gun?"

"Shoot foxes."

"Why?"

"Foxes kill hens."

I was glad he was going to shoot foxes, so that the cluckin' hen would be safe sitting up on the nest. My uncle said, "I get five shillings for every fox's tongue I take to the police barracks."

"Why do the police give you money for foxes' tongues?"

"The police want rid of all the foxes. That's why they pay us."

"Couldn't you keep showing the police the same tongue?"

My uncle laughed and said, "They've thought of that, they keep taking the tongues off me."

One day my aunt said, "Come to the henhouse till I show you something." I followed her into the henhouse. She lifted me up in her arms and said, "Look in the nest." I looked in and saw two wee chicks cheeping away. They looked a bit dirty but I thought they were beautiful. My aunt said, "Keep looking at that egg with the crack in it." I kept staring at the egg. I could see the crack getting bigger. Then a wee hole appeared. A wee beak was hitting at the sides of the hole. Soon the hole got much bigger and bits of shell were falling onto the nest. Suddenly, a tiny, dirty, wet chick fell right out of the egg. It started cheeping but not as loud as the others. It was probably exhausted after trying so hard to break out of the egg. I said to my aunt, "I just love them wee chicks, even the dirty, wet one." My aunt said, "Isn't God good?"

"What did God do?"

"I kept praying that the cluckin' hen would stay on the eggs."

"Where's the cluckin' hen now?"

"Out stretchin' her legs."

I was happy at my granny's. My granny, my aunt and my uncle loved me and were always hiding little treats under the bowls which were upside down on the dresser. I would find a few sweets or an apple. Sometimes there would be a few pennies to buy my own sweets.

At night, I would lie on the sofa, with my head on my aunt's lap. She would stroke my hair and sing to me. One song she sang was my favourite: *Play to me, Gypsy, the moon's up above. Play me the serenade that I love.* I would ask her to sing it over and over again.

One night, while she was singing to me, there was a terrific thud on the wall behind the fire. I jumped up. My aunt said, "Don't be scared, it's only Joe from the shop throwing a stone against the wall. He wants to tell us something." My uncle went out. Soon he came back and said, "Joe Furey's dead, the funeral's on Sunday." My granny said, "God rest his soul."

"Why didn't Joe come into the house with the message?" I asked my aunt.

"Well you see," she explained, "he's minding the shop and if he walks down the field from the shop, he can see if anybody is going into the shop, and can tell them he'll be back in a minute. He stands inside the stone wall and throws a big stone."

"Does Joe have a lot of big stones?"

"Just the one, we always give it back, for the next time."

I often went to Joe's shop for the messages. My aunt would tell me what she wanted. The last thing she would say was, "Get the restin buns". One day when I was eating a restin bun, I asked my aunt, "Why are these buns called restin buns?" My granny and my aunt laughed and laughed. Then my aunt said, "They're not called restin buns, Child, they're *Paris* buns." Then she said, "When I send you for messages, I know there will be a bit of change left over and that's why I say, 'Get the rest in buns.'"

They were lovely buns, bright yellow, shaped like a hill, wide at the bottom and pointed at the top. There were lots of little sugary bits resting all over them. I thought *restin buns* was a good name for them.

It was nearly Christmas. My aunt said, "Do you want to write to Santa Claus?"

"Will you write and tell him I want a pair of wellingtons that flap against my legs?"

"Wouldn't you rather have a doll?"

"No, just a pair of wellingtons that flap against my legs." There was a girl in my class who always wore wellingtons. I used to watch her walking and loved the sound the wellingtons made flapping against her legs.

On Christmas morning, my aunt came up to the bedroom with a cardboard box. She put the box on the bed, saying, "Santa Claus didn't forget you." I pulled the lid off quickly and inside was a pair of shiny black wellingtons. I took one out and ran my fingers along the shine. I jumped out of bed and put on the wellingtons. I walked proudly across the floor, but there was no flapping sound. I walked back again but still I couldn't hear a flapping sound. I sat on the bed and started to cry. I sobbed, "They're no good. I don't want them. They don't flap." My granny said, "There's nothing wrong with the wellingtons, it's your legs, they're too fat." That made me cry more.

Then granny said, "There's something else in the box." I rubbed my eyes with the back of my hand and slowly looked in the box. There was a piece of crumpled newspaper. I picked it up and felt something hard inside it. I opened the newspaper and there I saw a half-crown. It was shiny, it was for me - a whole half-crown for me. I held it up for my granny to see. "Half-a-crown all to yourself," she said "what're you goin' to buy with it?"

"Nothing for a long time," I said, "I want to show it to everybody first." I held it tight in my hand. Then I took another look at the wellingtons: when I got a chance, I would get a pair of scissors and cut the tops to make them flap.

My other aunt, who came to stay for Christmas, gave me a doll. It had a nice face, big blue eyes and even eye-lashes. The hair was yellow and curly. It had a pink dress, white socks and black patent shoes. The shoes had the same shine as my wellingtons. My aunt said, "Turn the doll over and press the middle of its back." I did and the doll said, *Mama.* I kept pressing it to hear *Mama, Mama, Mama.* I wanted to take the dress off and open up the doll's back to see what was making it say *Mama,* but I knew my other aunt would be cross.

We had goose and stuffing for our Christmas dinner. My other aunt was a cook in a big house, so she cooked the Christmas dinner. When the dinner was nearly ready, I told her, "I don't want any of that dinner. I just want mashed potatoes and butter." She looked as if she was going to hit me, then said, "You'll have what we're all having."

"I don't want anything then."

"If I had you," she said, "I know what I'd do with you."

My granny said, "Leave her alone."

My other aunt said, "She's ruined. She gets everything she wants. She should be home with her mother."

Everybody was quiet and I knew they were all in a bad mood, just because I wanted mashed potatoes and butter. I felt sorry for my aunt and my granny, so I said to my other aunt, "Alright I'll have the same as everybody else." My other aunt said, "Good girl."

My aunt told me that every Christmas Night there was a fire lit in the good room for the neighbours to come in. She said Joe from the shop would be able to come because the shop would be shut all Christmas day and night. There would be sandwiches, a big Christmas cake and plum pudding. She said the men would drink stout, the women would drink sherry and I would have lemonade. We would all be singing. I couldn't wait for it to be Christmas Night. The good room door was always locked, except when special visitors came.

We were all in the good room. Everybody was laughing, singing, drinking and eating. My granny said to Joe from the shop, "Now, Joe, give us a few verses of that old favourite of yours, *The Shandon Bells.*" Joe stood up and put his glass of stout on the table. He was standing with his back to the fire. He cleared his throat and started to sing. I noticed that the sound was coming out of his nose, not his mouth. It sounded funny and I started to giggle. My other aunt grabbed me by the arm and pushed me out through the door. She said, "Don't you dare show us up, Joe can't help it if he sings through his nose. Now you stay here 'til he's finished."

I stood outside the good room door, Joe was still singing but it wasn't funny any more.

Christmas was over. I felt sad because I knew I would soon be back at school. I thought that maybe the teacher might have died during the holidays. She was very old. If she had died, we might get a nice young teacher who would always be smiling and wouldn't wear black clothes. She would have nice black curly hair and wouldn't shout or rap our knuckles with a stick. But I knew my teacher hadn't died, because Joe from the shop would have thrown a stone at my granny's wall.

In school, just after Christmas, the teacher stared at us over her glasses and shouted, "Some of you are going to the headmaster's room for a reading test. If your reading is excellent, you will be moving to the next room in a few weeks.

I kept saying to myself, "Please God, let her send me for a reading test." I kept saying it over and over again. Suddenly, I heard my name being called and I jumped up. The teacher said, "Take your book and go to the headmaster's room." I wanted to run out of the room, but the teacher would be cross and would call me back and I might not be allowed to do the reading test, so I walked, but inside I was running.

I knocked on the door of the headmaster's room. A voice shouted, "Come in." I walked into the room. There were lots of long benches with lots of big boys and girls sitting on them. The headmaster was sitting at a big desk. He was smiling, I wasn't afraid of him. He used to play football with the big boys, at playtime and sometimes he would come over to the infant playground to talk to us. I wasn't afraid of the big boys and girls either. My sisters were there too, smiling at me.

The headmaster said, "Open your book and read."

I started reading. I was reading well and I was feeling happy. The headmaster said "Stop." I stopped. He said, "Give me your book." I gave him my book. Then he said, "Carry on reading." With my hands behind my back, I read on to the end of the book. "That's all," I said when I'd finished.

I could hear laughing and then the headmaster started to laugh. Everybody joined in and I started to laugh too. I didn't know why we were all laughing, but I didn't care. Then the headmaster said, "Quiet, everybody." He handed me my book back and said, "Tell your teacher you passed with flying colours."

I liked the way he said that, though I didn't know what *flying colours* meant. The word *passed* was the word I liked best.

I ran into my classroom, remembered where I was and walked slowly to my place. "Well?" the teacher asked.

"I passed with flying colours."

"Sit down," she said, "you're too old fashioned."

The scary feeling had gone. I would soon be leaving this room. I wanted to dance and shout and sing. I felt so light inside, I could fly like a bird - like flying colours.

ROSE MORRIS

Rose Morris was born in Altaglushan, Co. Tyrone. After graduating in Art and Design from Belfast College of Art and gaining her Art Teacher's Diploma at Birmingham College, she settled in Manchester with her husband, John, and family. She is Head of the Art Department at St. Gregory's High School, Openshaw.

Rose is the *Irish World Heritage Centre's* cultural officer and a founder member of *Manchester Irish Writers.* Her watercolours and photography have been shown at local exhibitions.

HOMELESS FAMILY
after Rembrandt's *Holy Family with Angels*

Always in this one room,
Can't lay my hands on a thing.

Haven't room to put a foot down.
Always stepping on something,
But not what I'm looking for.

I wish you wouldn't smoke,
It's in my hair, my clothes,
It's not good for any of us.

And stop that hammering,
You'll wake the child.

Them damn flies get everywhere!

THAT TIME

I never spoke to my father on the telephone,
Never wrote him a letter—
The height of foolishness—
New fangled things,
Never welcome in our house.
Few exchanges,
Rationed speeches,
Directives
Requests.
Shared poetry,
Childhood memories.
History,
Euclid,
Latin responses.
Left school at eleven and took the spade.
But he had caught in a single room
All the knowledge imparted
To a schoolful of pupils
By a fearful man.

How do you till the land,
Or harness a horse?
Learned that from Frank o' the Burn.
Paddy McGuinness timed his watch
Using Old Moore's Almanac and the setting sun.
Mark Patterson's cow calved.
It had two heads.
That was *before something* they said.
Uncle Edward had his house burned down.
He'd moved in after an eviction.
There was a priest in every house that time.
They were taught Latin by a man beyond Pomeroy
Travelled there once a week on a bicycle.

Should have gone to America—
Kathleen, Maggie, Bridget and Charlie went—
Got as far as Cork, came back.

ALRENE HUGHES

Alrene Hughes was born in Enniskillen, but grew up in Co. Down. She moved to Manchester when she was sixteen, where she now lives with her husband and two sons.

She teaches English in a Bury school and has been writing for about ten years. Her short stories and poems have been published in a number of anthologies. She is a founder member of *Manchester Irish Writers* and helps to run workshops and events for the group.

AUNT KATHLEEN

The key was of another time,
solid, black lead, portcullis big.
It grated in the lock of 73 Cregagh Road,
built in the year the Titanic
sailed down the Lough.

Aunt Kathleen kept school still
for great nieces brought to visit.
"Spell chrysanthemum!
Recite the four times tables!"

I knew her in her decaying years
when the mezzo voice
had risen to a scratchy whine,
and thick tresses
had thinned and yellowed.

Hard to imagine
that shrunken figure
now caged in her parlour,
behind the wheel of her shiny Austin seven:
The police-man on points duty,
holding up the traffic on Royal Avenue
for Miss Goulding to pass.

BALLYWALTER

Ballywalter, the Sunday school outing.
We draw up, slewing grit in front
of a mission hall, halo blue.
The sky sags to watch strange hands lift me down.
A low wind greets us, like a cat around our legs.

For a moment the lightness of panic
twists free, catches my throat,
'til Rhona McKee grips my hand,
runs me across the empty road,
dangles me over the sea wall.
My sandals touch seaweed slime,
find a toe-hold on the slippy boulders.
I pick my way to the sand,
watch waves, brown as stewed tea, lick and lap.
Squatting, I scrape sand with a cupped hand
squeezing its dampness to finger ridges
soft as the waves in Rhona's hair.

Afterwards, in the paraffin warmth,
sitting close, I stare at the
brown paper bags stained with grease,
wax straws in mineral bottles,
lick icing from the bun, suck
the straw flat and useless,
leave crumbs in brown lemonade.
Later, as rain thrattles the tin roof,
the gospel meeting begins:
Sunday songs I know and all the actions.
Jesus bids us shine. with a clear pure light.

Sometimes I kneel and press my eye to that
window on Lilliput, to peep again at
You in your small corner and I in mine.

A MISSED HEARTBEAT

Most people grow older with their past all around them. Family, friends, places accompany them through the days that slip from the present and tumble into the past. But not me. I got on a boat twenty five years ago and left my past behind like a pair of uncomfortable shoes.

Now I was going back. Through the plane window the coastline appeared, defined by the cold grey of the Lough. I tried to work out which town was which below me: the large one could be Bangor: the scoop of beach, Helen's Bay: wooded hills, Holywood; the shores of childhood.

It was the air, like a slap in the face, I recognised first. Stepping from the plane, it was sharp and clean, colder than Manchester. A mist ringed the hills and I thought of the old Belfast saying, *If you can't see the Cave Hill it's raining. If you can see it, it's going to rain.* I dipped my head as the rain needled my face. Aunt Kate was to meet me at the airport. Until we touched down, I hadn't given a thought to the fact that after twenty five years I might not recognise her, nor she me. I needn't have worried. She was there, nervous, twisting her keys, still large and well-corseted in a smart suit.

I moved with the crowd towards her. I knew she hadn't seen me in the sea of faces.

"Hello Kate."

She looked at me without recognition. Then her face lit up and she let out a shriek of amazement.

"My Goodness! I wouldn't have known you."

'Well, it's me alright." I hugged her. Up close the passing of a quarter of a century was evident. Deep lines etched her face and the auburn hair was now pale sand, but coarse and thick as ever. I touched my mass of red curls. Her eyes followed my hand.

"And where's all that lovely long hair?"

"Oh, Kate that was all very well when I was eighteen, but I could hardly have it like that in my forties, could I?"

She looked at me then: really looked, as though seeing me as I now was, a woman approaching middle age. She nodded.

"Aye... well... I suppose that's the way of it."

We drove away from the city following the south shore of the Lough. Sitting next to her in the car I felt... like a kid who'd been away from home for the first time. Why did I feel guilty? It was ridiculous. I had teenagers of my own. I was used to being the one driving the car, worrying about their guilty looks.

"What does Michael think about you coming over?"

That was a tough one. "Well, he was a bit surprised, but he didn't mind. It's not as if the boys need much looking after." In fact, Michael had been incredulous when I'd finally plucked up courage to tell him I wanted to go over to Belfast.

"What on earth for? You've always said you wouldn't go back, that there was no point. Right?"

"Circumstances change..." I said weakly and left the room.

The truth was there were reasons why I wanted to go back. Many reasons, but they were all tangled up in my mind like the scraps of wool my mother used to keep for mending. I had once spent a rainy afternoon untangling them, working patiently, following each colour to its end. Now I had to trace back the threads of my life undoing the knots time had tied. I'd lived in England longer than I'd lived in Ireland. Was it only the place name on my birth certificate that gave me any claim to Irishness? Whatever that was. Some would say I had only come back now that it was safe to do so, like some fair weather friend, and perhaps there was some truth in that, but I also needed to return to restore memories of people and places before they faded beyond recall.

The car swung through the narrow gates and into the drive. I'd always loved Kate's house. She'd had the money to buy new furniture and carpets when Mammy and I had relied on handouts and secondhand shops. In my teens I spent a lot of time at her house and I loved to wander around looking at pictures, ornaments and books, hoping one day I would own such things.

I stepped inside and saw it was the same—same furniture, same carpets and curtains but saddened by twenty five years' wear. It hadn't changed, yet it was so different. Kate showed me into the lounge and fussed about lighting the electric fire. It was a room for strangers. The smell of burning dust came with the warmth.

"Sit yourself down, have a wee rest and I'll make you some breakfast John'll be back soon. He's taken the dog out."

I didn't sit. I travelled back down the years. The carpet had faded, the tiled fireplace had cracked, but some things had endured. Great Aunt Martha's piano, bequeathed to Kate, stood against one wall, above it hung a water colour of Ben Bulbin. In the corner stood Gran's elegant bow-fronted cabinet and behind its leaded panes rested a generation of china and glass.

I wandered into the hall where the large mahogany barometer hung. When I was small I thought it controlled the weather—it pointed to sunny and the sun would appear at its command: a move towards rain and clouds would assemble over Black Mountain. As I reached up to tap it the back door opened. It was Uncle John. The kitchen door was open a fraction.

"Well...?" he said. I could hear him fussing with the dog's lead.

"Well what?" Kate was at the stove.

"Is she here?"

"Of course, she's here. I'm making her some breakfast."

"And what did she say then?"

"Och be sensible John! I'm not going to meet the girl off the plane and say, 'Hello, what are you doing here?'"

"Why not?" John was taking off his jacket. "Twenty five years, she never sets foot in the country, twenty four hours notice and she's back. Seems to me there must be some reason. Maybe we're all about to be invaded by long lost relatives with English accents."

I slipped back into the lounge. I should never have come. Moments later Kate shouted from the kitchen. "Come and sit in here. Your fry's ready."

The table was laid with a linen cloth, a plate of soda and wheaten farls in the centre. I'd forgotten how white soda bread was, how wheaten was flecked yellow like tweed. John joined me, stooped like an old man. He must have been nearly seventy but his face was ruddy and healthy as ever. He greeted me as though he'd seen me last week, asked about England like it was at the bottom of the street. I played the game and told him about the children as though he knew them, had watched them grow up. I spoke slowly and deliberately, aware that he was not picking up every word. I wondered if his hearing was going.

"You've an English accent." he said bluntly.

"I haven't," I protested. How could I have when in England my accent was queried by those who met me? But, my voice didn't match his. It knew the tune but the key was different. I'd heard talk of a mid-Atlantic accent. Could mine be mid-Irish Sea?

Kate carried the two hot plates to the table using a tea towel.

'There you are now. An Ulster Fry."

The plate was swamped with more grease and calories than I'd eat in a week.

"Ulster bacon and sausages," she went on, " Do you get them in England?"

I said something about it being Danish over there, all the while thinking I can't eat this, but I knew I'd have to, or risk upsetting her. The fried pancake with its yellow frill and the potato bread with its brown speckled skin hung over the side of the plate and fat was already dripping from them and congealing on the mat.

Later, when the family chat began to dry up, I felt restless. I wanted to walk the streets to see what I remembered, what had changed. Besides, the rain had stopped. "I'm going out," I said. "I'd like to have a wander around... you know..." My voice trailed off. Did I need a reason?

"You'll not get lost?" Kate asked, concerned.

I raised my eyebrows as if to say, "Come on. I grew up here."

She turned away "Aye, alright then."

It was a good ten minutes walk into the town. Now, as I came to its outskirts, I could see a roundabout and a dual carriageway sweeping in a lonely curve to ring the town. So the main road no longer ran through it. I followed the town centre sign. Around the next bend the land would rise steeply to my right and a drive would sweep up to the grey stone church. It was there, smaller than I remembered. The gates were chained, the railings rusty, the drive covered with weeds. It looked weary, alone. Its windows gaped darkly and the roof had gone. I crossed the road quickly, passing a row of tall thin pebble-dashed town houses. I had once gone out with a boy who lived in one of them, but I couldn't recall his name or which house was his.

I did however, remember the road next to the houses. I had last seen it on the T.V. news about ten years before. It had been cordoned off then, an R.U.C. officer standing warily at its head, his gun slung ready across his flak jacket. The report was about a body that had been discovered in the early morning—the camera had zoomed in on a wet green tarpaulin.

Next, the Police Station, sheer concrete, corrugated sheeting, sandbags, locked gates. I had gone to school with a girl whose father had been the town policeman. She'd lived in the Victorian building that served as station and police house. Their door had always been open and the front garden had marigold borders in summer. Had her home been swallowed by this concrete creature and did it still exist beyond the walls? Perhaps it did, but I knew for certain there would be no marigolds.

Halfway along the High Street I looked for the cafe, the haunt of my teenage years. Its speciality had been home-made ice-cream. On the pavement outside a six foot painted concrete ice-cream cone had attracted trade. Day trippers to Bangor would stop on their way home and sit around licking chocolate vermicelli before it fell with the melting ice-cream. The concrete cone had gone, but the pavement cracked and dipped in memory. The cafe was boarded up and the plywood daubed with para-military slogans.

The town was crowding in on me, places I knew yet didn't know, recognised, but hadn't seen before, like a distorted dream, a warped deja vu. It had been a mistake to come back, I knew that now. I wasn't naive: I had known it wouldn't be the same, but now I didn't want to see any more. I sat on the granite base of the war memorial and decided I'd go back to Kate's and ring the airport, perhaps I'd get on the late night flight. It would have been easy to cry sitting there. Big drops of rain began to fall from the low black clouds. A woman stopped in front of me and began searching in her bag. She pulled out an umbrella and as she put it up, she glanced sideways at me. She was about my age, perhaps a little older. I suddenly became aware of the possibilities. Had I known her in that other time? Was it possible to discern the teenager in the face of middle age? "Are you alright?" she asked, concerned.

I nodded and looked away. I couldn't face recognition, the questions, the catching-up. She moved closer.

"Do I know you from somewhere?"

"No" I said, "I'm not from here." I stood up. "I have to be going." I left her standing there.

The rain was falling in sheets, blowing down the street so I kept my head down. What was there to see? The town I had known had gone and in its place was an impostor, scarred and spoiled. I left the shops behind and walked in the shelter of a high, rough stone wall, pitted and yellow with lichen. The graveyard: one thing I knew would be constant, exactly as I had left it.

Her grave was at the far side near the sea. Inside the grey protective walls, clocks didn't tick, no one aged. I was eighteen and saying goodbye to Mammy. There was no need for me to stay. I had nursed her through the pain and I left her in peace. Left my country, too, as it began to explode and bleed and suffer. I could not witness another lingering death. Maybe I had been wrong then. Should I have stayed with it through its pain as I had stayed with Mammy?

"She would be glad to see you here."

It was Kate with a spare raincoat and an umbrella.

"I should have come back long ago." Then I added, "Or maybe I shouldn't have gone at all."

"Not gone! My God how can you say that? It was the best thing you ever did."

She took my arm and we went through the rusty gates towards the sea and began to walk along the shore path. The wind had dropped and the rain began to ease.

"I know you're wondering why I'm here."

She shrugged. "It's your home."

"I'm not so sure, Kate," I said and added, "Do you realise I've lived more of my life in England than here?"

"Sure that means nothing."

I didn't answer right away. I was trying to get the sentences shaped, ordered, to make it sound rational. The words had to be right and not just so that Kate would understand.

"I don't know where I'm from anymore. How can I be the same as you and John and all the people in this town, when I left you then and didn't come back until I heard there'd been a ceasefire." My voice held steady just long enough to add, "The place isn't the same. I don't belong here."

Kate stopped walking and faced me. Her voice was strong and sure like it had been when I was a child and she had helped me make sense of the adult world.

"Look, if I'd been your age, I'd have done the same, but my roots were too deep: I'd a job, a house, a husband. But you were just a girl, easily transplanted to another soil—given the chance to grow safely."

Maybe she was right. We walked a little in silence then sat for a while on a bench looking out over the Lough towards Antrim on the opposite shore. Cave Hill was obscured by cloud and the certainty of more rain was in the wind. The grey sea lapped on the shingle below us, just as it had lapped last week on the day of the ceasefire and on all those other days. The days of the Shankill Road bombing, Bloody Sunday, civil rights marches. It had ebbed and flowed every day of my childhood and all through my mother's life, back through the past, peaceful and violent times alike. Then, as now, it bathed and soothed a troubled land.

Kate stood up and smiled, "Did you know the park was still here?" She took my arm. The swings hung in their shipyard chains, the witches hat swung eerily and the slide rose up like Goliath. There were children there, too, singing as they played a skipping game; the next generation, one that, hopefully, would not know trouble, just the beauty of their country. Kate seemed to sense my thoughts.

"They'll have a childhood," she said. "It will be for them as it was for you. The trouble was only a missed heartbeat."

I caught a snatch of their song.

"I'll tell me ma when I get home..."

Just the same. Just the same.

I began to walk towards them. Maybe they'd let me join in. I knew all the words.

Alrene Hughes

AN IRISH BOX

In my box I will put
Irish linen embroidered with love
Dulse bitter and brown as iodine
The letter I from Kell's Book

In my box I will put
The sharp salt Donaghadee wind
Notes from Van's throat
A glimpse in a milliner's shop
in Victorian Royal Avenue

I will go with my box
To a high hill in Holywood
To watch the grey lapping lough
And Goliath's shadow

There, I will open my box
and wrap myself in Irish missed

IN GRAN'S KITCHEN

Gran in her kitchen,
Belfast Telegraph spread on the table,
Her finger moves down death's columns,
Stopping at a half-remembered name.

Behind her, two stoves.
One blind, white and mottled grey,
The other, black, flickering its red eye.
Deftly Gran flips its saucer lid
And slides in some slack.
Heat hugs us.
High on the mantle
A clock ticks hoarsely.

The gate rattles,
A worker's whistle
Busies the lazy air.
We turn, Gran and I,
Unhurried, unworried,
Even when a black face grins.

Frank eases the hump from his back,
Touches his dirty cap,
Steps into the warmth
To pass the time of day
And slips me a shiny sixpence
From a coal-grit hand.

CATHERINE MOLONEY

Born in Irlam, near Manchester, Catherine Moloney is second generation Irish. She worked for Salford City Libraries prior to having her two children. For the past year, Catherine has been living on the west coast of Ireland.

FOR JAMES

He's turned fifteen, a desperate age
To test the temperature of life.
Neither child nor man
Cocky but vulnerable
With a swagger that makes me smile.

He's listened silently hunched on the stairs
To the war-zone within his home,
Of Mother raging, pleading to be heard,
Oblivious of the child
Making a foray into bloody adolescence.

When did he grow so tall?
I must have turned away.
How I long to touch the now slender face,
But I do not dare.

I long to have back my sunshine boy,
But he's gone with his childhood—
All I have are discarded toys
And the old red jumper that comforted him
More than ever I could.

CATHERINE BREEN

A native of Gorey, Co. Wexford, Catherine Breen has lived in Manchester for twenty years, and is a graduate of Manchester University and the University of Huddersfield.

In the seventies, she had some poems published in Ireland, and read on R.T.E. *Coming Home* is her first published short story.

COMING HOME

I was on a steep hill and found myself almost running down it.

I had been worried about coming back, but need not think of that now. I felt fresh and light and free. The air was pure and still; so terribly still, with a hint of the sea. Further down I would pass the cemetery. The thought had been with me since I had arrived at the station. It had been strange not seeing her there, waiting for the train to pull in.

The cemetery gate was open. Half-consciously I began to wander along the narrow gravel path. The smell of the freshly mown grass drew me like a memory. Suddenly a head bobbed up from behind a low wall. The face turned to me. With a start I realised it was Andy, who worked there. The wizened face, still clutching a pipe between its teeth, smiled to greet me.

"Oh it's you again. Back for a visit then?"

"Hello Andy. Just dropped in for a minute."

"You're welcome. And tell me d'you know where your mother's grave is?"

"Oh, I'll find it."

"Gimme a minute an' I'll go along with you."

When we got to the grave Andy took off his hat respectfully. "She had it hard," he said, "God love her. Left a widow at a young age and you to rear too. She was a good woman, God rest her soul." Then smiling he turned, "Ah they're all great in here—never have a cross word between us."

I felt Andy's light mood lifting me, and tried to respond in like manner, "I see you're still smoking," I teased.

"Ah bedad I am," he said, "an' still alive—the only one here." He put the hat back on his head, smiled and limped away. He was an old man who spent his days here, tending the graves of people he had known, greeting the occasional visitor. It was even rumoured that he often slept in the little hut at the back.

Kneeling down I tried to pray, but Andy's words kept running through my head. His speech and easy manner reminding me of what I missed. Meeting up with him had eased the moment.

I looked around and began to take stock of where I was. In the distance, down in the valley, the familiar outline of the town. I had been thinking of this moment for a year, preparing for it, planning, but now that I was here, I could only re-acquaint myself with my surroundings: the low hills with their soft contours, the evening sun clinging to them. I sat on the grass and let the mood take me.

Gradually I began to take in the names on the headstones. They were all familiar to me, all known since childhood.

Others of the same names had been left behind and would be buried here too. Glancing through them was like taking in a view that never changed.

Next to my parent's grave, I was surprised to see the name *Downey*. Yes, it was John Michael, better known as Jack, my mother's old employer. How had I missed it last year, when I was here for her funeral? I had not known that our family graves were so close, but was glad of it now, felt it comforting. I had liked Jack Downey.

Alice was waiting for me. As we shook hands, I noticed a faint flush on her cheeks. She seemed anxious. For the first time, I realised how old she was. She had never been one to hug or kiss, but suddenly I wanted to take her in my arms and hold her very tightly, whisper that I loved her.

After an embarrassed moment, she turned away with a nervous laugh. "You look well Marie. Stopped off at the graveyard, did you?"

"For a minute. I met old Andy. I was surprised to see him, he's gone very feeble."

"Ah, drinks too much, that's his problem. Seldom goes home to his wife, I believe. She's always giving out about him. You sit down now and I'll get the tea."

Alice was my mother's cousin, had been her closest relative. She had lived alone for most of her life. Now she was my one anchor with this place.

"How's everyone in London?" Her voice came floating in from the kitchen.

"Everyone's fine. Brendan's busy at work. That's why he couldn't come. John's got a summer job at last, and Niamh's on holiday with friends." I knew she wasn't listening, seemed preoccupied.

I sank back into the comfortable old chair. The house was as I remembered it, everything in its place, and the carpet, though worn, covered with the usual protective rugs. I knew if I went into the kitchen, I would find the floor-tiles similarly covered with old newspapers. Sinking further into the old chair was like settling into a familiar place, finding it a perfect fit.

"I got a lovely bit of strawberry jam today," Alice was saying, "home-made by the Phelans. You can have some of it now with a bit of brown bread. You always liked my brown bread with a bit of jam." She had come back into the room laden with the tea tray. I got up to help her fix it on a small table close to both of us.

"Are the Phelans still there?" I asked, "the old couple I mean." I had forgotten about them. "They were cousins of my father, weren't they?"

Alice nodded, busying herself with the tea.

"It's strange, I've never felt any closeness with my father's family."

"That's the way your mother wanted it," she said, handing me the cup of tea. "Kept you to herself."

"I suppose it was because I was an only child. But father's people weren't very good to her, were they?"

"Oh it wasn't all their fault" She sipped her tea slowly; placed the cup back on the saucer. "After your father died, God rest his soul, she cut herself off from them."

"They hadn't wanted her. Didn't think father should have married her. She always said none of them came to the wedding."

"They weren't asked, Aleanna." The sudden sharpness in her tone alarmed me, rattled the cup I was holding. "It wasn't everyone knew your mother," she added, in the same sharp tone.

The dark was beginning to fall more quickly. It was mid August. In the garden the faint glow of the street lights, reflecting on the trees, caught the beginnings of Autumn.

"I suppose we never really know our parents," I said awkwardly, "I hardly remember my father."

"You were only a child."

"Mother said he wasn't like the rest of the Phelans."

"Well, she was right there. Jim was the odd one out. She used to say, you were like him, trusting, always prepared to see the good in people. But I don't know about that."

"What was he like, Alice, my father?"

"Oh he was a quiet man, very gentle. Suffered a lot with his lungs."

"I missed not having a father and she was very much alone. That's why I always felt I should have been here with her more." Alice had turned away, was looking out at the garden that was becoming restless with shadows. I wanted her to go on talking, connect me with the father I had not known. I had not realised how much I needed that: what a gap his death had left in my life. "It was great of her letting me go to University—all the sacrifices she made for me. Jack Downey always admired her for giving me that chance."

"Well he would, wouldn't he?" Alice retorted. Again the tone alarmed me.

"Why, Alice, why do you say...?"

"So as they could be together... you know..."

I did not know. My mother and Jack Downey? "But he was..." Married, I wanted to say, but the word would not come.

"He had a sick wife, always ailing, poor woman. Oh, they're all gone now, God rest them."

Tiredness was showing in Alice's face. The conversation had taken a sudden turn, and now I felt adrift. This holiday was not going according to plan.

Alice's girlish chuckle, half ribald, half comforting, broke in on my silence. "Child of grace, don't say you didn't know..." Her voice had become more soothing. She had always used that expression when she had wanted to comfort me as a child. The night was warm, the kitchen door had been left open and a pleasant breeze was coming in from the garden.

"When did his wife die...?"

"Oh she lived on for years as an invalid, died about ten years before him."

I was relieved at that, wanted to keep my mother respectable. No matter what the world was like now, I still wanted her to be the embodiment of the values she had passed on to me.

"Did they live together...?"

"Your mother and Jack? No, child, she would never have that. She worked with him; that's what the public saw. At least that's how she tried to keep it, but you know this place. It all came out when his wife died and they started going around together. They had a good life you know."

"He was never around when I came home."

Alice was chuckling again. "Oh you know how she was, prim and proper to the end. He knew his place. Keeping up appearances meant a lot to both of them."

"Why did she never let me know?" I felt betrayed, mistrusted. "I'd have been pleased for them, surely she knew that?"

Alice was silent.

"Was he there. . . I mean when my father was alive?" As soon as I'd said it, I felt alarmed.

"She was working with him then of course, had been for some time. Your father was a very delicate man." The last words hung in the air. I waited.

"When Jack died, she told me she had something special to tell you. Jack hadn't been well for months and she'd worn herself out looking after him. After his death, I left her to recover for a while. When I mentioned it to her again, she said there'd be a letter for you with her will. Then God love her she went so quickly, I suppose she hadn't got round to it."

I felt raw and tender, my skin so exposed, the air hurt. "What was it Alice? What did she want me to know?"

Questions were rushing into my mind, but how could I get them out in any order? Straightening up, I turned in the chair and faced her. I could see her outline in the dark, against the background of the high chair. It was like confronting a ghost. I knew then what that ghost was.

"Alice, who am I? Who was my father?"

"We were close, your mother and I, almost like sisters. But there was always a distance. Many times, I asked her right out, but she'd never say. Always insisted your father was your father, I mean the man she married. Oh God you know what I mean—I'm confusing myself now. She was a deep woman."

"Alice," I pleaded, I couldn't let it go now, "please. You used to tell me you had a special feeling about each baby you delivered, an intuition. What was your feeling... what was your feeling about me?"

She gave a tiny laugh, pleased that I had remembered.

"Please, Alice, what was your feeling when you first saw me?"

"That you were not a Phelan," she said quietly.

It was enough. I knew her words were true. I felt a calm I had not known before, a sense of being at ease with myself, as if my life had been a journey to this moment. Then I felt a sense of loss—and anger. Anger against the mother who had deprived me of the father I might have known, who had lied to me...

"They were good company, came here every Sunday night," Alice was remembering, "we used to stay up all hours, talking. We had some great laughs." She got up and began to busy herself with the cups. "I miss them both."

"I'm sorry, Alice, being away I've got out of touch. It must be lonely for you here."

"Oh you know me. I've got used to my own company. And health-wise I haven't done too badly. Maybe God left me for a purpose——to clear the decks before I go. Now, you know as much as I do. Your mother kept her secret."

"That's what hurts. She deceived me. God! the way I used to feel so guilty because I thought I was leaving her alone. She knew and she let me go on feeling it. She let me go on all these years not knowing who I was—and I might never have known. Alice, why did she do it?"

"We can never tell what drives others," she said softly, "but we can guess. She was a very possessive woman, and Jim's early death made her more so. It was her nature to be that way."

My mother had love, but had excluded me from it. I was a child of that love, but had never been allowed to know. All my life I had felt an outsider. She had kept me that way. She had given me that place in her life and I had never questioned it.

Alice moved closer and switched on a side lamp. She looked straight into my face. It was a look of concern and deep affection. "God love you, Child," she said, "you look like you'd seen a ghost. Don't take it that way. You know she loved you—very much. Maybe there were things she couldn't face in her own life..."

She placed her large, soft hands on mine. I felt their warmth. This was the first touch I would have felt on entering the world. This was the woman who had delivered me, who had laid eyes on me for the first time, who had washed me, wrapped me, cleared my eyes. Now she was clearing them again. I was being reborn, trying to find my own voice, to speak for myself, probably for the first time in my life. I thought of Andy in the graveyard, drunken Andy, as Alice had called him. My mother had been a good woman, and she had been left with me to rear. But I could no longer trust anything that was said about her. What did I know about her now, after all the years I had known her? And who was I? Finding myself would be painful; I would have to go through that. Then, and not till then, could I let the tears fall, the tears that had refused to come all this night.

In the light from the small lamp, I could see Alice's old lined face. I reached out to her and threw my arms around her. This time she was not embarrassed. Her big arms encircled me; her strength surprised me.

"You'll tell them all about this night, won't you, Child of grace? Let them know about their roots here—the quare lot we were."

Later that night, much later I left her. But before going, she had given me her instructions—everything in a small, neat box.

I know now what to do, when the time comes.

DECLAN McCOTTER

Declan McCotter was born into a family of nine, on a farm in Kilrea, Co. Derry. He attended Crossroads Primary School and St. Columbs College, Derry, before graduating from Manchester University. He currently teaches mathematics at Xaverian VIth Form College.

Married, with two children, Declan has been writing poetry for about five years.

GENERATIONS
to my father

You never became a grandfather.
Once, in the vegetable garden,
You looked up from the weeding
Between the rows of spring onions.
"Try that son," you said.
I put my tongue to the dandelion milk
And knew then
Each temptation of the big city.

Now I am far from that farm,
With Rory, and no vegetable garden.
And as I clear away the litter
Near a dandelion, I recall:
I never knew my grandfather
But you told me once
He'd been to the big city.

DEATH IN THE COUNTRY

The rope tightened to a muzzle,
He slipped and slid on bent hind legs,
Unaware of the swinging hatchet.
The last squeal soon drowned
In the plump of boiling water,
The sharpening of gullies.
In the light of tilley lamps
Sleeves rolled; they scrubbed, shaved and slit.
I peered, helpless, intruding,
In the steamy ancestral kitchen.
They wheeled wallops, red, white and purple
Where foxes sneeze.
He hung, rigorous, dripping.
A six-inch nail replaced the legal bullet.
They moved, cleanly, through dewy grass
To breakfast in nineteen fifty-nine.

Their bellies pressed crisp grass.
The silent stare split their breaths.
He approached brightening the fog,
Stepped onto gravel, day work done.
"I think they know about my report."
"Your tae's ready."
They waited, coldly, unsure.
Figures moved in the kitchen.
He reappeared. The harp flashed, gold on green.
A clinical click, a squeeze. A single shot.
He spun, sprawled, head thumped the bonnet.
Her last scream soon choked,
In their running engine.
He lay, she straddled.
They moved, quickly, through hedgeland,
Where snipes sleep,
To supper, in nineteen seventy-five.

PARTING COMPANY

You could tell there was more to it
Than reverie; he couldn't speak
And the red round the whites of his eyes.
A broad-shouldered man from Leitrim,
His back not so squarely against the wall,
Staring for long, blank moments,
His memory fidgeting,
As he turned the glass
Between fingers and thumb.
Leitrim, maybe, he was dwelling on,
A small farm and laughing youngsters.
Self-restrained, mannerly as usual,
He shifted himself slightly
When I questioned him again.
"How's things, how are you keeping anyway?"
"I lost a brother the day, fifty seven—"
The conversation lingered awhile
Then relapsed into silence.
When we parted company outside
Shaking hands, l realised
That what keeps us in the circle
Of our being, in the big city,
Is our being there,
Far beyond the fields and hills
Of our common childhood.
And as he moved off
Alone along the dark side-street
Towards the main road,
It became a lane they'd travelled down
So many years ago,
The buildings rising around him now
Like headstones to a way of life.

LEARNING IRISH

It's a long road there's no turn in.
Words not heard but seen one night
Tramping a short-cut through the bog
As darkness lowered in the *Gaeltacht.*
Eleven, and alone but for the mists
That were never there, had slunk away
When you arrived in new terrain.
At the end of the *rodden* a breeze
Came shivering through the rushes
Drawing a ripple across still pools
Deep as the child's imagination
Where he lay awake on nights like this
The door ajar to the old stories.
Coming to life again out there among
Sedge and heather, wisps of bog-cotton,
Stumbling, falling, rising again
From wet mosses that took his weight
Then sprung him free; like his tongue
Venturing now, finding its depth
In a language buried deep within him.
A language from across the border
Where bogland whispered the same words
As ancestors, gathered like shadows
Around the hearthstone of learning.

Gaeltacht: region where Gaelic is spoken

Rodden: pathway; from the Gaelic *ródán,* a little road

STELLA MARIE HINCHCLIFFE

Stella Marie Hinchciffe had her name chosen by her Irish grandfather, who had a lifelong love of the sea. As a young man, he had come from Dublin to work on Salford Docks, and had settled here.

Stella has written since childhood, when relatives and friends were regaled with her fortnightly *magazine*. She gained a Diploma in Graphic Design at Salford School of Art and Industrial Design, where she began to be influenced by the *Liverpool Poets*. But it wasn't until years later, as a mature student, on a creative writing course, that writing became a serious preoccupation. She has had work published in magazines and read on local radio.

PEARLS

Nested in blue velvet
they lay,
deep as cobalt
blue as rivers at Giverny,
string on string
of chained melody
captured in their
black hinged box:
my grandmother's gift.
She said she was given them
when she was my age;
she thought I'd like them—
I said I did,
my fingers caressing
their moon-milky surface,
shivering with joy.

I told the red-haired girl
my secret, standing in the
cold, grey concrete yard.

'Bring them,
bring them'
she begged, curls dancing
'Tomorrow,
tomorrow.'
I did—
delirious,

'Didn't I know they were unlucky?'
she asked,
her fingers caressing
their moon-milky surface
inquisitive with glee.

And,
in that moment
they seemed unlovely
their melody discordant.
Spoilt,
I spilled them,
kept them
like guilt
captive
in their black hinged box.

METAMORPHOSIS

Distanced by an ache of traffic
the world waits,
lulled by time, locked out
behind the windows of my childhood.
Within, my past has become
my present.

Taste of chalk catches memory,
etches reflections, which flicker
on the glass screen of innocence.
Dust motes, mottled, freckled by sun
shiver, hover, like musty ghosts,
huddled beneath grey slated roofs
slanted in shadow.

Silenced from children's chatter,
the room lies hushed, wrapped with
whispers of half-forgotten voices.
Yesterday's child,
white-socked, school-frocked,
plays violin to haunted corridors.

A door clicks, a telephone rings.
A bell beat of relayed rhythm
which jars my senses,
summons me, not to the concrete yard,
isolated from the hand which held me,
but to another time, another place
where I am mother.

A tree, beyond the sill, towers,
grown in absence to maturity.
Budded by blossom, she spreads
familiar fingers, plays shadow-dances
with an awakened breeze in
echoes of another Spring.

Winter's leaf clings to her fingers,
unable to let go. Sunbeams
polka-dot posters, already aged.
Silver, light-sprayed spider webs
hug the ceiling.
Out of reach they shield their
lace-dressed frailty.

ROOTS

I turn the switch—
'News at Ten'
shots which stir my conscience
crackle of burning timber
searing blaze of hate
the mindless feud lingering
on in age-old battle
fresh as today's headline
the brutal blood drowning the doorway
the valley of Gurtaderra

As a child
I listened
as my Grandfather
told tales
of winding bays
Derry Vale
salmon
leaping in the Foyle
of his emerald bride across the water
her pearl-pale tresses
winding
binding
my auburn hair around his fingers

I turn the switch—
in safe and easy exile
I do not understand the ancient quarrel
lie wakeful under labouring stars
voices everywhere
like rain
or sleet
or snow
another house
breathing its life into mine

SEÁN BODY

Seán Body was born in Templeglantine, Co. Limerick, and has lived in the Manchester area since 1956. A social worker, he has worked for Manchester Probation Service and the Social Services Department. Latterly, he has run a training consultancy specialising in child care.

A committee member of *Manchester Poets* and a founder member of *Manchester Irish Writers,* he is editor of *Tarantula Publications.* His poetry has won several prizes and he has won the *Irish Post* short story competition.

A collection of his poetry, *Witness,* was published by *Tarantula* in 1995.

BRIDGES
for Finn Deloughry

The Shannon Bridge is crying tonight.
A thin wind running a wet finger
round its steel rim wails

like our history; takes you down
streets you knew like a slash of the heart.
Good places to leave from.

A random hand of destinations dealt out
piecemeal: Quebec, Oslo, Kuala Lumpur,
a Bristol dustman, a priest in Sarajevo;

one who drew the short straw:
you put a flower on his grave.
But voices you hear are further back,

meld the contours of geography:
the map of inhabitations you carry
on the tip of your tongue.

Like Heaney's bogland,
each layer you strip
has been camped on.

You are more than historian:
a teacher who loves the feel of stories.
They need space to breathe in:

come by remote hills, old settlements,
evacuations, warm slowly
at the fire of attention.

I have forgotten the leisure
of whole nights to pass,
expressions that find me raw,

like a shaft from the opening door
and sudden
slip between the ribs.

I leave you to wait the bus
to Droylsden, *the valley of the dry
stream:* another history, ponder

how a way of telling can,
like a scent from childhood,
blast the senses open.

Seán Body

THE DART

The child you once were floats up to the broken windows.
We remain in the shadow of the chestnut
> John Ash, *The Burnt Pages*

Dublin Area Rapid Transit. Neat
as an acronym. Eye on the target.
Neat too its un-native sense
of urgency, time pressing...

The woman standing on Raheeny station
has time on her hands, lets it slip
through slow fingers. An anachronism
in tropic yellow dress, flowered hat

and sensible leather shoes that mark
a territory others do not encroach on:
the small pale of shadow they skirt
with bright confidence. Someone has left

her here. The list of her body suggests
an absence, the half-listening inclination
she wears like deformity. They bewilder
her, these light leave-takings.

Her goodbyes are sombre, inarticulate
as those I remember: the diffident migrants
for whom travel was an exposure.
Those awkward adolescents on the edge

of cramped seats, their careful bundles
clutched to them like confidences,
the train's movement lulling, dulling
the incommunicable sense of loss...

Forty years on, I'm thumbing the burnt pages,
remembering how, night falling, we watched
Ireland's Eye go out, our passage whip
the indifferent ocean to a white rage.

MIST OVER HOWTH

The bowed heads keep close
to walls, hug boundaries. A cold
mist shoulders back the day.

In the muted church, a single light
keeps faith; soft as a breath,
animates a hand, a face.

If you should turn away, O Lord,
how should I bear it?

The coffin descending the slow aisle
is too small to bear
on shoulders.

So light she seems
he would run with her
through the stopped town,

headlong the promised years:
play sand castles on the beach,
laugh in tossed waters.

Then brought up sharp,
she would scrutinise him
with her candid child's eyes.

She has transformed him,
his three months daughter.
Gravity has entered his boy's frame:

an acolyte in her ceremonial,
descending stone steps,
outstretched hands still

as if they touch wonder,
tender the small white coffin
ribboned like a bouquet.

O'CONNELL STREET

Legless in Dublin. You can be forgiven
a sick humour when all you've got
to stand on is your arse. Perched here

be the fountain of life: Anna Livia
herself taking the waters, an' a fine broad
she is, shafts on her like an ass cart.

What wouldn't I be doin' with them now!
The floosie in the Jacuzzi. Now the hoor
in the sewer, partial to empty cans, stale

bread, pigeon droppin's an' the occasional
rubber. An' wouldn't the man himself
be making great art of it. He's down

Talbot Street, leanin' on a stick,
with a hat that's up to no good—Me?
Sure that'd be tellin'. No accident,

Misses. Unless you count bein' born.
Come out like this, half finished. God
on his uppers. Or maybe just frigged-off

with all the shaggin', downed tools.
Champion of the workin' man: that's Jim
Larkin drawin' himself up to his full height,

arms beseechin' *Rise Brothers, rise!*
You'll always be shite if you let 'em shite
on you. Got it in one, James, like the pigeon

anointin' Daniel O'Connell's noble pate.
Not bad for a culchie, Dan. Won us
emancipation. Like all we elevate endures

bein' shat on. Ask Charles Stewart Parnell.
He's above where the ways part: politician,
patriot, orator. *All an Irishman needs*

is his eloquence. Had a spot of bother
with a mot, so we left him to the bed he'd made.
Couldn't' be havin' us liberated be a libertine.

We're forgivin' of the dead. Built him
a fine monument. And a square to himself.
Over there, the GPO, bullet-scarred

and ponderous: a proper place for poets
and revolutionaries. *Irishmen and Irishwomen:*
In the name of God and of the dead generations...

Ireland's seven apostles (not the full
complement) signing up for their memorial.
Of such indiscretion we are born.

Widest street in Europe, they'll tell you.
Never believe an Irishman when he's tellin'
the truth. We're carriers of history, a lost tongue.

A European city now, the past a commodity,
saleable as a tinker's prayer—Not a bad pitch
for a beggar. I do alright. I'm legitimate.

A man with no legs. You can't fake that.
What you see is what you get. This is me
in me stood up sittin' down

your own
Johnny-I-hardly-knew-you
sweet as a peardrop.

THE MASK

Black on black—in this night how do I see? I reach out and draw it away slowly, a thin veil, delicate as dust.

Listen to the children, Wendy. Hear how they laugh.

I don't want to hear, Mama.

Don't be silly, Child. What nonsense you talk. Listen, they are happy. Hear how they enjoy themselves.

I don't want to hear, Mama.

*What **is** the matter with you, Child?*

Please don't go, Mama. O please... Stanching the flow of tears with a clenched fist. *I love you, Mama.*

And I love you, Darling. Now go play with the others, there's a good child.

I'm the best runner in our school, Mamma.

Sure you are.

Miss Graham says I'll win the school prize.

That'll be nice.

An' the high jump. I can jump higher than the boys, Mama.

Yes, Dear, now go play with the others.

I don't want you to go, Mama.

Don't be silly, Child. I don't know what's come over you lately. I've got to go. Now pass me those earrings will you.

Please don't go, Mama.

I've got to, silly. Now pass me the earrings.

The earrings, Mama?

The earrings. And I wish you'd drop that whining Mama.

Yes, Mama.

The earrings... Come on, slow coach, I haven't got all day.

I like your earrings, Mama.

Glad to hear it. Now, pass them will you. God! look at the time. I'll be late again—do you want me to get the sack?

I want to run, Mama.

Then run, Child, run. You want to run. Okay. Fine. Run! You're the best runner in the school, you'll get the school prize. Great! Wonderful! Marvellous! Now show me. Run off and play with the others—and get from under my feet will you!

Will you watch me run, Mama? Will you?

Sure, I'll watch you run. Glad to. Just get started will you. Okay? Come on then... Ready? On your marks, get set—come on, one, two, three, go—I'm watching... I'm watching, Wendy... I can't see you go... I can't see... Have you gone so fast I can't see...?

I don't want you to go, Mama. O Please don't go... please, Mama... please...

*Just what **is** the matter with you, Child? I'm damned if I know!*

I don't want you to go, Mama. Please don't go, please...

I've got to go, Child, can't you see I'm late already. Now you be a good girl and run on...

O please let there not be another... this time please... Black on black and the dry laughter... Again and again. Clawing at it with rawed fingers. Uninhabited skull holes gouging darkness, deeper and deeper. Again and again... Black on black and the dry laughter... O please, this time, please...

"Wendy? Wendy! Wendy!!"

The voice is far off, alarmed. A man's voice, pleading, accusatory. I wake slowly into bleeding arms.

"Sorry," I plead foolishly, "sorry..."

"I couldn't wake you," he accuses, "you wouldn't hear..."

Black on black. Beyond the darkness, darkness. A small light shines in through the blank window, it has ice in its probe.

"I'm sorry..." My finger nails have gouged deeply into his flesh and blood is trickling in little angry scrawls down his thin arm. "Sorry..."

With what tenderness, I might have kissed those small wounds, caressing them with tears of repentant love, an intimate Magdalene, cleansing in his anointing. Instead I say, "Sorry..." The sound disturbs the room momentarily, like a stone dropped into a pool, generating little spurts of shock.

Out of bed, I put on my dressing gown, wrap it around me like a shield, feel it encase the cold. The light has gone and the window has turned in on the room, which seems as if nothing will stir in it again. Then I feel his closeness, sense it—the tentative movement from the bed, stopping. "Don't touch me," I scream at him, " don't touch me..."

"I..." his weak, hurt voice falters, stops. Silence fills the room.

I need not have done that, demeaned him, soiled his clumsy concern. "I'm sorry."

"Bitch!"

The angry word lets in the air, pushes back the predatory silence. As if a window has opened, I feel its sharp relief.

"I didn't mean..."

The wounded, thin body, hunched in anger over the pillow, seems to have taken my place, ugly and vulnerable now. In its hopelessness, it seems to be craving persecution. I watch it with a remote, careless understanding.

"Bitch! Bloody bitch...!"

Words and silences and old hurts picked up like stones to hurl. I draw the cold tighter.

Later, I will hear him crying in the other room, secretly, desolately—wait for the thread to break, the bond to wrench.

The small card on the mantelpiece has lost its whiteness, turned to buff. *Telephone or call in complete confidence.* The last word has become indistinct, its letters half obliterated, confidence faded.

The woman who answers the telephone speaks like she is holding a glass. "Can I help?"

"My name is... my name..." To say who I am, establish the me. *Wendy:* a small sound I come to.

"When would you like to come in?"

"Like...?"

My hand is tight in a little fist like a child's, knuckles boring into my other palm, grieving, wounded. I have said the name, mentioned him.

"Your stepfather?"

"My mother's boyfriend," I insist, refuting the contamination of a relationship.

This place I have come to, this small space partitioned off, in which I sit opposite a stranger, is like a box within a box. I want to tell him how significant this is, how I feel anticipated.

"What age were you?"

Age? I cannot remember. I know the years when it must have been. "Between ten and thirteen," I tell him, "I can't remember exactly." I give a little laugh, feeling selfconscious, a little foolish. How could I not remember? Am I lying? Does he think I am lying? Minimising the guilt, my part.

I look at him, not directly, obliquely from my waist, where I keep my gaze: long fingered hands on the table, veins becoming pronounced, gold flecks still lingering among the changed hairs, up the quiet sleeve, shoulders bent, head turned, intent, greyed hair.

"Why can I not remember?" I raise my face to his, half meet it, flinch from the steady, permitting eyes.

"Can you tell me about it?"

The voice is so soft I want to cry. It confuses me, a soft, unfamiliar voice—another man come to heal, gentler, stronger, undemanding. *This is our secret. No one must know. No one.*

"I remember the terror and the isolation." Had I always felt loneliness? Had it drawn me to him? *It's alright, pretend I'm your father.* Trembling in the chill of eyes. *O Please... please don't make me...* Going home by a circuitous route, knowing only he would be there. Through empty places, not wanting to think of what might be waiting. *O Please...* Back entries, brick walls, barred doors, climbing up over the sewer pipes, exhilarated. I liked it there: a wasteland tomboy. *You should have been a boy. I think you are a boy. Let me see if you are a boy, let me... No, no, no... O please no...* Take off my school uniform and dress in jeans and sweater. Cut my hair short and hide my eyes—maybe then he won't want me.

"There were sewer pipes somewhere near where we used to live. They keep coming back to me... I was a bit of a tomboy." A little laugh has come into my voice, affection for *her.* "I loved clambering over those huge pipes." He smiles too, reacts to the child, the innocent memory. *Ah! what have we here then? What is this little hideyhole?* Why does the scream not come? Why does he not hear it?

Why does it not shatter around him like breaking glass. *No,* is all I say, weakly, too late, knowing he will not be restrained. *Not a boy then?* The mockery in that voice is ugly. I want to hide from it, to close my ears and not hear, not hear it ever again and not see. I think to kill him, when he is not looking; to put a knife into him. But I know the voice will not stop, will still be there—in me. *Not a boy then.* Not a child.

"Sometimes the memory stops... cuts off." It does it now: I feel the apprehension, the sense of confusion, of enjoyment and stalking menace. I feel the sun's brightness—not its warmth, just the troubling light, the blindedness, the closed silence and voices far off.

"Apart from that I don't have any *memories...* my whole childhood... just voices and feelings. It's as if my childhood exists only in those voices..." I look again at the unthreatening hand, the still fingers, try to guess at the waiting eyes: a new silence. "Not much to re-create me from." I laugh nervously, foolishly, half denying. "I have never said that before," I mumble awkwardly.

"Is it true?"

I nod quietly. No need to deny... to be ashamed... to pretend I exist. I feel very tired, exhausted as from a long climb. "I suppose I wanted..." What I was about to say has drawn me up sharp. I fidget, flinch from it, trace a scar down my right index finger, feel it sore from the pressure of my nail, feel the sweat drop from under my arms, erupt across my breasts, down over my stomach—I feel the hard unflinching invasion, tremble.

"If I let him..." I had forgotten that voice, but recognise it instantly, feel confused, want to hide from its trusting, to turn away.

"If you let him?"

"Maybe he'll like me."

I resist the temptation to stop her, to cut her off. Entrust her to him, a stranger; surrender her like a infant I have been holding and cannot comfort.

"Maybe..." The voice is small, plaintive, devoid of hope.

"I could have run away... told someone..." I stop, acknowledging the lie, surrendering, leaving it naked.

"You did try."

That startles me, I know I have not said it, admitted, accused...

"To tell someone."

My fingers crack, the chair moves. The sweat is cold across my breasts, down over my stomach. She would not have believed me. Would have thought I was lying. Blamed me.

"It would have hurt her."

"Your mother?"

"She loved him, needed..." But I say no more, leave it in the air like an accusation, the greater terror. "I loved her."

"Loved," he repeats, emphasising the tense.

I had not meant to imply that, hear myself deny it angrily, selfrighteously, then admit, "Loved." As I say the word my voice peters out with a kind of sad finality. It is the way I remember all the words between us, dying finally in a small unheard plea. "Things aren't good between us," I tell him. Then I feel I have betrayed her—her deafness exposed, her preoccupations. "She tries," I tell him, trying to explain, to redeem something, to say, I love her. "Now I think she has given up. We're strangers. I suppose I blame her. She was my mother." Again it is the angry, plaintive, vengeful voice of the solitary, unnoticed child. I admire her, want to cheer her lonely, tenacious anger, and her joy, the sheer delighted physicality of her scramble over the pipes, running down an incline that always caught her up in its momentum, bore her away, out of control, out of hope of stopping before she smashed into the grey towering wall; and then at the last moment saved, drawn up like a horse at a fence, her breath rasping and breaking as she returned to its thrill.

"He killed me..." I resist the compulsion to laugh nervously, self deprecatingly, softening the impact. "Killed the joy in me." And I die again of shame and pain, the ugly smile and his contamination pumped into me. I feel it hot and vibrant coursing through my being, corrosive, putrefying. It's stink assails me, even in the bath I cannot rid myself of him. I try to scour him out while she complains outside the locked door. *What are you doing in there, Wendy? Why have you locked this door?* I think she will smell him through the door and cower in a corner, my legs pressing in on each other, trembling.

"I expect people to know. On the bus I used to sit away from people so they wouldn't smell him..."

"You still feel this?"

"Yes." The room is small and confined. Piles of old clothing and toys are stored in a corner and against the dividing wall which separates it from a similar one next door. Occasionally muffled voices or the slow movement of feet break through its thin insulation. Further away, somewhere in the bowels of the building, a telephone is ringing unanswered. I keep willing someone to pick it up, but it keeps on ringing, insistently, uselessly. Two of the walls are covered in children's drawings, stuck up haphazardly with pins or Sellotape. One of them is of an empty room with a closed black door. It is outlined in heavy, angry crayon and all its lines converge in an acute angle in which the door is set, distorted, out of proportion. An enormous black knob gives a feeling of impenetrable loneliness.

"I might have drawn that," I say.

The room smells of its confinement, of abused spirits, of others shedding their pain and contamination, of children crying, of loneliness and isolation. I look again at the child's drawing with its hard cold lines: a child and not a child. I know her.

"I used to feel so alone, so abandoned..." The telephone has stopped ringing. I wonder if it has been answered or has just given up. In the next room someone is crying.

The ugly room chokes in on me and I want to run from its clamped poverty, its repository of odours, from the stink and bafflement of its pain and shedding, its grey walls and ugly paintings, like discarded selves grovelling in a mire of defeat and recrimination—half formed, mutant. The crying stops and starts and stops again like waves rolling over tired shoulders; the sound is raw and ugly and insistent. And the telephone is ringing again, seems to start up in mid note, as if it had been taking a breath. *Hear the children, Wendy. Hear how they laugh.*

Tears are in my eyes now, and behind them they press like a hard ball. I hold them back with terror, increasing the pressure I no longer feel able to control. If it breaks, I know I will be crying for ever, so I let its excesses trickle down my clamped face. "I'm always dribbling," I tell him, smudging the pain across my cheek, feeling my own touch like a stranger.

"And never crying," he says.

Again the soft, unflinching voice is a permission, an incitement. And I see *her*, the child, small and frightened and trusting, turning to me, craving my understanding—my forgiveness.

"It's me that wouldn't listen," I say, "me that blamed her, me that wouldn't forgive."

"You were a child."

"I still think I'm *her* inside, that the rest is phoney." I put my arms around myself and hold *her* very tightly, but when I have stopped crying, I say, "I don't like me much."

Outside I feel relieved. A wind is rising, invigorating, playful. It sweeps a piece of old newsprint from the street and drops it casually at my feet. I look down and read: A BUMPER HARVEST. I kick at it and it is swept away.

Three o'clock: an hour before the traffic begins; three hours before it is safe to go back. I have no fondness for Goodbyes. I feel cold. Two tramps are huddled in a doorway. One of them is feeding scraps to the other, who keeps bowing in little curtsies of gratitude. When they have finished they get up and walk away in different directions.

The newspaper is back at my feet, wrapped around them like a twist of rope. Then it is swept up again and spirited down an adjoining street, where it wraps itself round a street light.

The wind has cleared the civic gardens of all but the homeless: dotted in little insular huddles around the sparse shelter. An old man keeps staring at me, first with suspicion, then with disapproval. I feel his old starved eyes exposing me.

"Fuck off!" an old woman keeps muttering under her breath. I think she has forgotten she is saying it. I smile collusion, an unasked for empathy. She does not notice.

A man with one leg is lying out in the grass, careless of the cold. A bottle of whisky is where his leg should be.

I get up and walk away, followed by the old man's angry eyes. I want to turn back and speak to him, tell him I am sorry—sorry for the ugliness I have brought into his eyes.

The light is out. Safe. I fumble for my key and let myself in.

The fire has been lit and the table is set for one. A warm smell of stew is coming from the cooker. Nothing else seems to have been disturbed, yet already the room is empty.

The note on the table says:

I LOVE YOU
Richard

Bastard! I feel assaulted by his meekness, his left behind
love—another ghost. Another violation. Turning the
other cheek—and the knife.

"I love you, you bitch," he'd said, humiliated, self pitying;
the hard anger massed against him, invincible. "How long
do I have to go on taking it?" his voice hoarse with defeat.
"How long, Wendy? How long do you have to go on
humiliating *him* in those who care for you?"

A feeble "Sorry," to say goodbye.

The dream is late.

From a corner of the darkness, I sense it first, feel its
still presence, wait in quiet anticipation.

I have become accustomed to its slow appearance, not
gradual but delayed, like in darkness where my eyes take
time to adjust.

Only the mask is visible. It is convex, roughly meshed,
the cheeks bulge like a doll's and have large white circles
that turn slowly to grey. The eye holes are deeply set,
shadowed, blank. A thin paste-white nose reaches down
to the small clamped mouth.

Nightly it comes to me in this way. Nightly I reach out
and peel it away, only to find that behind it there is
another and then another, all with the same expression
of desolate mockery, the same lonely ambiguity.

I reach out to it now, take it gently in my arms, cradle it.
Behind it there is nothing. I feel it's cold vacuity. It is so
fragile, I tremble as I stroke its white-grey cheek, softly,

inquiringly. Slowly, I begin to rock to the stroking and cradle it deeper and deeper in my embrace.

"Me," I am whispering to it, "me..."

A tear squeezes from its blank shadowed eye, trickles haltingly down the still face.

GERTIE

At first it was little things.
Forgetfulnesses: a kettle left to sing,
appointments missed. Eccentricities:

shoes unmatched, hat at a raffish angle.
Took midnight strolls. Returned to streets
that had changed while she was out,

fumbled keys in strange locks.
Bewildered by kindnesses, took tea, smiled
at faces, questions, strange wallpaper.

Recognitions came and went
as if a wind getting up swept them
like confetti through her mind.

Slipped from their moorings,
her thoughts are all at sea.
Waves sudden as laughter

rack the pensive face,
the small window she tightly closes.
Absence settles in stale rooms,

becomes presence.
Strangers come occasionally,
wrestle the stiff gate,

the rusted latch, linger
irritably, faces distorted
with the ache of words.

She is calm, smiles at their insistence,
the mouths forming O's
as if they would howl at the moon.

scríbhneoírí

manchester írísh wrírers

Manchester Irish Writers was set up two years ago and from very small beginnings, has become an enthusiastic group of ambitious writers, at various levels in their development.

We are very fortunate that two of our members, our co-ordinator, Alrene Hughes and Seán Body, editor of *At The End of the Rodden,* have brought to the group experiences of being involved with other writers' groups and of having had stories and poetry published. With their encouragement and guidance members have gained enormously in confidence, which has resulted in the publication of this collection of stories and poetry—a long term aim achieved in a relatively short time. We wish to thank them very sincerely for their unstinting support.

As well as providing focused workshops, the group meetings are also social occasions, where much pleasure is derived from sharing thoughts and ideas—and memories. The group meets on the second and fourth Thursday of each month, in the Irish World Heritage Centre, at 7.30pm. New members are always warmly welcomed.

Beig céad míle fáilte roimh gach uile dhuine.

Rose Morris
Cultural Officer
Irish World Heritage Centre